HANNAH'S
Heart

HANNAH'S *Heart*

A Believer's Journey Through Infertility

NAJIYYAH BAILEY

Get
WR TE
PUBLISHING

Hannah's Heart, A Believer's Journey Through Infertility

© 2017 by Najiyyah Bailey

All Scripture quotations, unless otherwise indicated, are taken from the King James Bible Version.

ISBN: 978-1-945456-94-7

Printed in the United States of America.

Cover Design: Kevin Vain– CoLab Creative Group
www.colabcreativegroup.com

Editors: Akira Frierson, Linease Bethea

Photographer: Kasi McKoy, Studio 15 Productions
www.studio15pro.com

Printed in The United States of America

TABLE OF CONTENTS

DEDICATIONS

To the Most High God, who has given me every good and perfect gift, I thank You for every blessing and every trial. Thank You Lord for answering my prayers and using me to showcase how great You are. There are not enough words in the human vocabulary to express how grateful I am; for the way you saved and called me, protected and provided for me, forgave and comforted me, and for loving and caring for me. Thank You Lord for this infertility journey that allowed me to draw closer to you.

To my dear husband, my high school sweetheart, Allen Bailey, for loving and supporting me in all that I do. Thank you for being a listening ear, a shoulder to cry on, and for allowing me to share this portion of our journey with the world. Thank you for making me laugh when life makes me want to cry. Even with the crisis we went through while writing this book, you encouraged me to finish. I love you and thank God for allowing me to share time and space with a man He made just for me. Thank you.

To my loving Pastor, Rev. Tracey L. Brown, for being obedient to God, preaching countless encouraging and comforting sermons. The message, "My Condition is Not My Conclusion," along with many others strengthened my faith and changed my mindset to believe God for the impossible. Thanks for your loving support and for being the best pastor in the universe. Your perseverance and commitment to shepherding God's people inspires me to press on. I am blessed to call you my Pastor.

To my publishing coach and mentor, the midwife herself, Rekesha Pittman, who has taught me to master my projects, pushed me to write, encouraged me to complete every assignment, and has mentored this young woman to get to the finish line. Thank you for sharing your many talents with me.

To my Divine Divas Sisters for encouraging me along this writing journey, and for giving me the best support and advice along this motherhood journey. I love you all: Audrey, Phyllis, Nicole, Shonte, and Sonya.

To my mentor and friend, Rev. Georgette Bush, who encourages me with the most beautiful words followed up by loving actions. Thank you for making me family. To my late mentor, Rev. Danielle Bush, for fanning my flame, igniting me in my gifts, and for prophesying to me at the mountain top that joy, peace and happiness was coming before the end of 2011.

To Rev. Dollie Hamlin and to Sis. Sheila Logan for being obedient, sharing with me what The Lord told you to speak into my life: that I would soon be a mother. Thank you for declaring what thus saith The Lord.

To Apostles Chris and Angelica Montgomery for helping me through the publishing process. Your generosity made this book a reality. God bless you!

To my DEW family, thank you for your encouraging words. Shaquana and Stephanie, you have been my covenant sisters in this season of writing. Thank you!

To my "I Believe" sisters and brothers, I thank you for sharing your stories that helped me understand that I am not alone. I dedicate this book to you all. I give a special dedication to Rich & Tajuana Allen and Ellis & Tina Still.

To Cynthia Frazier, who supported me when she didn't even know me, and who has been a true representation of the love of Christ. Thanks for encouraging me my sister.

To Tonya and Renee, I thank you for sharing your children with me. Thank you for allowing me to take part in motherhood. This is a gift that I could never say thank you enough. Thank you and I love you both.

To my late grandmother, Madeline Smith, who taught me how to be a loving, God-fearing mom. To my late mother, Janet East, who loved me with all her heart. To my loving Auntie, Ann Timmons, thank you for supporting all I do.

And to every woman and couple who has been or will go through the infertility journey, I dedicate this book to you to remind you that you are not alone.

INTRODUCTION

Hannah's Heart was downloaded to me in the middle of the night. I could not sleep that evening and I knew that something supernatural was going on in the air. I'm not sure if you've ever experienced God waking you up during the wee hours of the morning, but it is, often times, a spiritual experience. I started praying and I heard God saying, "Write the book, tell your story." I started praying even more, asking God what should I write? At this point, at age 33, I had been through many experiences - some good, some bad, and some things I should have lost my mind about, but God! So still I wasn't sure what I was supposed to share. I went further into prayer and then began to receive the names of the chapters that I would write: Divine Plan, The Secret Garden, Ain't I A Woman, Don't Give Up On God, They Just Don't Get It, Get Drunk,

Elkanah's Love, Lord Remember Me, and Unspeakable Joy.

I never dreamed that I would speak to people about my experience with infertility let alone write an entire book dedicated to the matter. I recall one of my prayers, when I asked God to bless me with a baby. I took after Hannah, one of the greatest prayer warriors in the Bible. I look up to Hannah because our stories are so similar. But I remember that I promised God that if He blessed me with a child, I would dedicate the child back to Him, that I would bring that child up to know His Word, that I would raise my child to know that Jesus is Lord, and that I would tell the world of what an awesome God He is.

What better way to glorify God than to share with others what He has done for me? The purpose of this book is to first, testify of the goodness of Jesus. Secondly, I wrote this book to encourage those who are struggling with infertility that God has not forgotten about you. It is my desire to share my story in order to provide hope for those who think they are alone. And lastly, I wrote this book to provide family members and loved ones, who may not understand or have insight on what barren women and couples are experiencing so that they can support and help without being insensitive to the struggle. This is a major reason why barren women and couples do not share what they are going through. My desire is to begin a dialogue between the fertile and infertile so we can continue to help one another as we go through.

This book talks about how faith works and how God answers prayer. It also discusses the love of God and how you can get to a place that you can trust Him with all your heart. As a worshipper and lover of music, I found that on my saddest days, it was music and scripture that lifted my spirits. In each chapter, you will find a meditation scripture, prayer, and songs that personally helped me get into the presence of God. I ask you to write down your reflections after each chapter. What is God saying to you specifically? Please write down the words so you can revisit them to comfort you on the days when you need it most.

I pray that this book will allow you to press into the presence of The Most High. Meditate on the scriptures. Listen to the songs. Say the prayers out loud. I believe this testimony will allow you to see and understand how God can and will turn things around for your good. Enjoy, be free and be blessed!

Chapter 1
DIVINE PLAN

As a little girl, I would line up my baby dolls and pretend I was their mother. I have fond memories of playing "mommy" at age 3 with a newborn baby doll along with a yellow baby tub and a small piece of Ivory soap. I would clean that baby up, like my mommy did for me, wrapping her up in a towel to dry her off and keep her warm. I think most girls, like me, dreamed of being a mom. Even as a girl child, raised by her grandmother because of her mother's addictions, I promised I would never allow anything in life to cause me to abandon my child. When I was finally given a diagnosis for my infertility, it was devastating. Dreams became interrupted and visions were shattered.

Graduating from college, being successful in your career, getting married and having children are life events that many of us hope to one-day reach. Not in any particular order, but there is something about these milestones that some of us believe will validate our success on this journey we call life. These events are often met with celebrations and congratulations no matter what culture or background you were raised in. These chapters in life are oh so familiar to us no matter what our background is, no matter our ethnicity, no matter our religion or belief system. Most children find their identity in their family structure and when we become adults that identity shifts into the families we create. What happens when some of the life events we may have planned for ourselves do not go as we planned? Have you heard the saying, *"If you want to make God laugh tell Him your plans?"* I believe we plan and hope for the best in our lives, not to be out of the will of God, but because we do not understand how we can be truly happy any other way. In my experience, nothing went the way I planned it and infertility put a major halt in the design I had conjured up in my imagination for my life.

I know you've heard people say it time and time again, that God's plans are not our plans. This statement is not just a cliché or another scripture. This declaration is true and it speaks volumes to us. Although we cannot see how the heartache of our struggle can be for our good, understand that God is using it all for our good. Let us examine the plans God had for our sister Hannah, found in the Book of I Samuel.

Hannah's struggle with infertility was planned by God. The bible says nothing about Hannah being punished by God but it is written, that the Lord shut up Hannah's womb. Why would God send barrenness to this woman? Through Hannah's prayers and tears you can see that it was her heart's desire to give birth to a child. Like us today, Hannah felt disgraced from this inability to give life. It looked hopeless for Hannah. Her husband Elkanah loved her anyway and her rival Peninnah

God decided to make a distressing impossibility a miraculous reality.

taunted her daily. I imagine everyone that surrounded Hannah unanimously decided she would remain childless. But God, He had a plan all along to bring forth rain in the desert. God decided to make a distressing impossibility a miraculous reality. A great prophetic voice would be birthed from a once barren womb, the great Prophet Samuel, whom Hannah dedicated to be set apart for the Lord's service. That day when she wept loud and did not eat, Hannah could not even imagine what God was planning to do through her.

No matter what season you are in at the current moment, know that God is able to do things beyond what your human mind can comprehend. If you knew the things He had planned for you it would literally blow your mind. Even if you are in a season of weeping and not eating like Hannah, know that God has a plan for your life. His plan is not to harm you, His plan is not to hurt you. His plans are designed for your good and to make you prosper.

There is a divine plan for your life even as you tread the waters of childlessness. As I sat in my OB/GYN's office at the age of 19 to receive a negative diagnosis, I would have never guessed in a million years the blessing God would send my way 10 years later. I often quote the psalmist saying, "it is good for me that I have been afflicted; that I might learn thy statutes."

Infertility has driven me to my knees and drawn me closer to The Lord more than I would have on my own. It caused me to feel an emptiness that drove me to search for a Savior that would fill up the space with love. Without this journey, I would not have sought the Heart-fixer. Without this thorn, I would not have searched for the Great Physician. This obstacle in the plans I had drawn out for my life may have been a major interruption in my design. But the obstacle was God's perfect divine plan that would bring me joy and push me to do what He was calling me to do. His ways are not our ways and His divine plan is so much better than our carnal intentions.

Meditation Scripture:

"For I know the thoughts that I think toward you, saith the Lord, thoughts of peace, and not of evil, to give you an expected end."

-Jeremiah 29:11 (KJV)

Prayer:

Father I pray that you would help me to understand that you have a plan for me. I don't know what your plans are, but I trust You and declare today that I know You love me like no one else could ever love me. And because You love me, You have good intentions for me. Help me to release control of my issue and to commit my infertility to You. You know every pain I feel and every tear I cry, so Lord be by my side through it all and give me a peace that surpasses all understanding. In Jesus name, Amen.

Song:

"Thy Will" by Hillary Scott

Reflections

_____

_____

_____

_____

_____

_____

_____

_____

_____

_____

_____

_____

_____

_____

_____

_____

Chapter 2

THE SECRET GARDEN

I made a decision to conceal the truth so that no one else would be able to know my innermost thoughts and feelings. I could not bear to even say it. I hid the facts so that others could never judge me for anything that I was lacking. No, I wouldn't tell a soul. I disguised the reality of my situation so that I would not even have to form my lips to say the words that cut me so deep: You will never have children. If I told it, it became real. I had to keep that a secret to avoid facing my reality. I thought that no one would understand. I convinced myself to keep it a secret. I just would not tell anyone.

Struggling with infertility is not a joyful topic of discussion nor is it a great subject to discuss over dinner. It is not the type of conversation that can break the ice among a group of strangers and it is not the kind of banter you'd want to have among even the people who you are closest to. The truth is many women, and even men, are dealing with the reality of not being able to conceive. We hide in dark corners hoping no one finds out our issue. We find clever ways to answer that infamous question that is posed often a few months after getting married: "When are you guys going to have a baby?" We give answers like "When we're ready" or "Maybe in a few years" or "We just want to enjoy each other first." We give these common answers as opposed to the truth that it is actually a struggle for us. Why do we hide this predicament?

Sometimes I wished that people would just mind their own business! I wanted to scream at the top of my lungs when people asked when I would have a baby. My husband and I, high school sweethearts, were married in March 2008. Since we had been together for 9 years prior, people were waiting on us to have a baby immediately. Allen was the only one who actually knew my secret.

Since the very tender age of 16 I had known that child bearing may be a problem for me, and I kept it a secret for years. I had reached my peak of puberty without ever starting my menstrual cycle. I thought I was a freak of nature. "Don't tell anyone of this, you'll be the laughing stock among your friends," I thought to myself. Maybe one day, you'll be normal, you're just a late bloomer is what I would try to convince myself of. But then I turned 17. And then my 18.th birthday came, still nothing. I graduated high school and went on to college. I was now 19 years old, a full-time student with a part-time job and car of my own, transitioning into young adulthood...and still no menstrual cycle. My condition was such a secret, I had not told Allen until we were 3 years into dating. I heard my friends talking about motherhood, unplanned pregnancy scares, how many children they wanted when they got married, etc. I would throw in a line or two about having children one day, pretending to be normal, but all the while holding onto the secret that was tearing me a part inside.

Everyone who is on this infertility journey has a different story. Some have unhealthy ovaries, some may have pelvic disorders. There are some who suffer with issues related to the cervix and others who have disorders or diseases that make conception difficult. I was diagnosed with primary amenorrhea: the failure of menses to occur by age 16 years, in the presence of normal growth and secondary sexual characteristics. I had never met another woman who shared this diagnosis, but it was my reality, and I never even dreamed that I would tell a soul. While many women can identify with the Woman with the issue of blood we hear ministers preach about on Sunday morning, I was the woman with the issue of no blood. The doctors said they couldn't be sure, but I was probably born with an absent uterus. Statistics say it is a birth defect that happens for an unknown reason in less than 2% of girls born around the world.

Regardless of the diagnosis, we feel ashamed, so we hide. Another reason we want to stay hidden is fear. Even though some of us stand firm in our faith and we know that God has not given us the spirit of fear, we fear what others will think of us. We are afraid of what people's reactions might be. I was so troubled at the thought of not being able to give birth to a child, I could not imagine growing older, dying, and not leaving my legacy through my own blood. I really had my mind set on things here on earth, and not on things above. I always wanted to be a mom, so the devastation of knowing that may not happen was overwhelming. I kept my secret because I feared the worst thing in my life was happening to me. The one thing I most desired would never happen.

Another reason we keep it a secret is that it guards us. The secret guards us against judgement from others. It guards us from having these painful conversations with people. Whenever I would look at a diaper commercial on television, I was drawn to tears. How could I ever talk to someone in real life about my issue? Keeping the secret makes it easier to pretend everything is fine. Keeping the secret eventually became natural. It became the greatest defense mechanism.

Hiding something is keeping it in darkness. The enemy loves to do his work in the darkness. While we hide our conditions, the enemy continues to tell us the lies that keep us in a constant state of grief. When we try to conceal what is going on in our hearts, the devil will try to manipulate us to believe that there is no one to find comfort in. In darkness, there is despair and anguish, but in the light, there is joy and freedom! Don't stay in the dark, be free and enjoy the light. I understand that it is not so simple. I recall the first time I ever revealed in public that infertility was something my husband and I were going through. I was asked to share my testimony at a Women's Ministry service as a newly married woman. No one

In darkness, there is despair and anguish, but in the light, there is joy and freedom!

knew what I was going through, yet I believe people understood that a newlywed would have a testimony about how the Lord was keeping her marriage. I may have been randomly picked but God was setting me up for my deliverance. I remember thinking to myself "What will I share?" I prayed and asked God to help me with my words. God said loud and clear, "Tell them about how I am keeping you through barrenness." I was scared beyond words because I had never shared my infertility issue with anyone. When the day came that I was to share my testimony, I remember being so nervous. I walked to the podium, grabbed the microphone and opened my mouth unrehearsed. I simply said that I was grateful for the opportunity to be a wife, that

God was helping me understand what being a good wife was, and that God was protecting us and keeping us as we were two young people entering the real world of adulthood. I began to say that not only was the Lord keeping us as we faced the challenges of being newlyweds, but God was keeping us through infertility. I went on to share that the issue was such a heartbreak for us, but God is with us through it all, even on the roughest days. I gave God the glory and asked that they pray for us as we went through that journey. When I took my seat, as the congregation clapped and shouted their "Amens", I felt a weightlifting liberty that I had never experienced before. I realized that I had revealed my condition and I was not met with judgement, but rather, I was met by the support of the saints. They generally believed with me that God was going to bless me with the desires of my heart.

Now I am not saying you will be met with this support every time you share. However, Holy Spirit will reveal to you what to share and when to share. Releasing will not only be your liberation but it will be encouraging to another couple who is suffering in silence. Transparency is needed for deliverance. I needed to be delivered from the shame I felt. Speaking about my infertility allowed me to begin to develop the faith I needed to inherit the blessing that God had already planned for my life. Come out of the darkness. Tell of the goodness of Jesus, even before your prayer is answered.

Meditation Scripture:

" Strengthened with all might, according to his glorious power, unto all patience and longsuffering with joyfulness; Giving thanks unto the Father, which hath made us meet to be partakers of the inheritance of the saints in light: Who hath delivered us from the power of darkness, and hath translated us into the kingdom of his dear Son."

–Colossians 1:11-13 (KJV)

Prayer:

Dear Father God, the One who knows all of my strengths and weaknesses, Lord I ask that you help me to come out of the darkness of my brokenness and step into the light of freedom. Lord I pray for a courageous spirit to share my condition so that You may be glorified and that the enemy may be horrified. Help me to understand that I must come out of darkness into the marvelous light and that You are light in the darkness, My God, that is who You are! In Jesus name, Amen.

Song:

"Way Maker" by Sinach

Reflections

_____

_____

_____

_____

_____

_____

_____

_____

_____

_____

_____

_____

_____

_____

_____

_____

Chapter 3

AIN'T I A WOMAN

Infertility is defined by the World Health Organization as "a disease of the reproductive system defined by the failure to achieve a clinical pregnancy after 12 months or more of regular unprotected sexual intercourse." When you are dealing with the harsh reality of the fact that you have the inability to conceive and have children, it makes you feel less of a woman. I thought to myself, if I could not give birth to children I am worthless. I want to encourage you that your abilities or your inabilities do not define who you are. Your current circumstance does not limit you from being everything that God has called you to be. No matter what you are going through and no matter where you may be on your journey with this thing called infertility, remember that God has a plan for you and that plan has been designed for your good. He has a plan that is meant for your success and it is not meant for your demise.

If we were to be honest about it, we would say we feel shame about this issue. We are ashamed and embarrassed that we cannot simply have children like everyone else around us. There is a sense of disgrace we feel in this condition that makes us feel unworthy. I have felt so worthless I thought about taking my own life. If I could not have children, I didn't feel like I had any purpose in my life, so why should I still be living?

One day, after work, I was driving in my car feeling depressed. There was nothing in particular that triggered my sadness, it was an everyday feeling for me. As I was driving down the mountain of Berkeley Heights, I would pass these beautiful homes that rested on this large rocky land. I could see the entire city of my hometown from up there. I thought to myself, "just keep driving straight, go off the road and just let the car crash. Najiyyah you are worthless and you have nothing to give anyone." As I began to put my foot on the accelerator, I heard the voice of God say, "I love you." I pulled over and cried a deep travailing cry, asking God to take away this heartache. Why couldn't I just come to terms with it? Why must I have this desire to be a mom if I'm physically unable to? My prayer was "Lord, just take away the desire and heal my broken heart."

Our worth in God's sight is not determined by what we can or cannot do.

Like Hannah, I cried and grieved, and grieved and cried some more. Feeling unworthy of living simply because I was barren in the natural. Driving down the mountain that day was a shifting point for me. I had come to terms that this issue was not because God did not love me. He reminded me that I belonged to Him. I want to encourage you that The Lord cares about you. He allowed you to be here and that means you have purpose. While man may define us by our capabilities, our worth in God's sight is not determined by what we can or cannot do. God loves us just the way we are.

Hannah felt like a disgrace. Her rival Peninnah made sure that she remained in her state of depression by provoking her. The bible does not go into detail with what Peninnah did to Hannah exactly, but I imagine that she must have teased and taunted Hannah. Perhaps in the mornings she would nurse her child in front of Hannah. Or even more insensitive, say loudly to her children "you look just like your father!" The two wives could have gotten into an argument over housework but it escalated to Peninnah saying "he may love you, but I give him many children." Some of us may or may not have had a Peninnah to deal with. But many situations we've dealt with have felt like what I like to call, a "Peninnah encounter". A Peninnah encounter consists of a situation that you are met with that reminds you that you are a childless woman surrounded by those who are blessed with children. These encounters can feel taunting while going through them. When the Gerber commercial comes on television and we should furtively excuse ourselves from the room because we are driven to tears; when we go to the mailbox, and have to open yet another baby shower or gender reveal invitation; when your teenage cousin announces she's knocked up for the second time; when you hear your friends talking about pregnancy scares; when you see someone mistreating their baby; when you hear on the news a young mother kills her newborn infant, etc. There are so many situations in our everyday lives that may include a Peninnah encounter. Although these situations were not strategically aimed or in any way personally directed towards us, sometimes it feels as though we are being teased.

These encounters often lead to us feeling less than a woman. God's knowledge of you is perfect. He knows everything about you and created you with greatness in mind. Despite your childlessness, "you are fearfully and wonderfully made in the image of God" (Psalm 139:14). Your situation does not define who you are and it definitely does not determine where you are going. Hannah may have had her encounters with Peninnah, but she was still Elkanah's wife and she was still indeed a woman. No taunting or teasing could change Hannah's position in Elkanah's household. She was still the wife whom he loved. Her inability to conceive a child did not change who she was to him: his beloved. The same is true for us, in who we are in God's sight. We are God's beloved; and He loves us, not for our inabilities, not for our shortcomings, not for our illnesses, and not for our conditions. But the Most High God loves us because He created us. He knew what your infertility issue would be and He doesn't love you any less because of it. You are a woman. A woman who was created by God for His glory, a woman who will not be consumed by the things of this world, a woman who is destined for greatness, a woman created on purpose for a purpose.

Never forget that you are a child of The King and that you are a joint heir with Christ. As my pastor, Reverend Tracey L. Brown would say, "your condition is not your conclusion." God loves you unconditionally. Your condition could never change His mind about you. You are a woman. God's grace erases our disgrace.

Meditation Scripture:

" The LORD your God is in your midst, a mighty one who will save; he will rejoice over you with gladness; he will quiet you by his love; he will exult over you with loud singing."

-Zephaniah 3:17 (KJV)

Prayer:

"Father, thank You for loving me. Help me to see me the way You see me. God, I want to be able to receive Your love and all the benefits that come with Your love. Lord I want to believe that I am loved by You, no matter what my condition is. I love you Lord and I know You love me. Allow me to understand that I matter, and that I have purpose, and that you have greatness in store for me. I am loved because You are love. I adore You Lord. In Jesus name, Amen."

Song:

"I Am What You See" by William Murphy

Reflections

_____

_____

_____

_____

_____

_____

_____

_____

_____

_____

_____

_____

_____

_____

_____

_____

_____

_____

Chapter 4

Don't Give Up On God

Even as little children, most of us were encouraged to dream big. We teach young people to shoot for the stars and be whatever you want to be when you grow up. Our realities are often overwhelming when we compare them to our dreams. Aspirations that have developed from the passion in our hearts are sometimes met with difficulty that we never imagined would hinder us from reaching the goals we had in mind. But I say that anything worth having is worth fighting for.

Becoming a mom was something that I always had a desire to be but the reality of my diagnosis put a halt on those plans. Sometimes I would just ask God to take away the desire but then other times I would pray for a miracle to happen. My attitude in prayer was somewhat double-minded since I could not see how God could do this for me. I have learned through this journey that faith is a key factor to obtaining anything that you ask of God. "Faith is the substance of things hoped for and the evidence of things not seen" (Hebrews 11:1). At times, the "not seen" element hindered my ability to believe, but faith is actually something that you cannot see. Some days it was almost impossible to believe God for my baby.

It is written in Mark's Gospel that *"whatever you ask for in prayer, believe that you have received it, and it will be yours."* (Mark 11:24, NIV) In this text, Jesus is trying to get His disciples to understand how important it is to have faith. Faith is something that will benefit the disciples even after Jesus leaves them. He's trying to get *Believing is a requirement for receiving God's blessings.* them to realize that faith is the key. Today, understand that faith is the key to unlock your miracle! As the disciples are excited to see that the fig tree has most definitely withered as Jesus had cursed it earlier, Jesus responds to them in verse 22. If I could remix this verse when Jesus says, "Have faith in God" I would say "You didn't know, you better ask somebody!" They did not fully understand who Jesus was and He had to let them know that when He said something, it would surely happen. Oh, if we could just follow our Savior's example and call those things that are not as though they were.

Believing is a requirement for receiving God's blessings. Yes, it is a requirement and not a request. The scripture above teaches us to believe so we may receive and that there is no faith in the receiving. Faith comes before receiving what God has for us. God is saying that it is faith that will move mountains, it is faith that will change your situation, and it is faith that will allow you to see the manifestation of what you've been asking for.

At times, our grief can be so consuming that it tries to overpower our belief that God is all powerful. The pain can be so heavy that we forget that God is able to do anything. The Bible says that Hannah was "in bitterness of soul." Yet, while she was in this state of grief, she had enough faith to ask God for what she truly desired, a son. Although the Father knows our heart and knows what we stand in the need of, we must present our prayer requests to Him. We are to make known all of our supplications and even better yet, cast our cares on Him. Being childless was one of the heaviest burdens I ever carried. It was only when I completely handed it over to God that I would feel the weight lifted off of me. This took great faith! Handing your burden over to the Lord means you totally relinquish control of the situation. Releasing the burden means you trust that God's will be done (and that is scary)! I sometimes would ponder, what if God's will meant no child for me? Another element to relinquishing a burden and totally trusting God means we must wait.

To wait means to strain your mind in a certain direction with an expectant attitude. To wait means to look forward with assurance....so will you wait on the Lord? You must decide that you will look forward with assurance to what He has for you! Declare that you are straining your mind towards God with an expectant attitude! (Isaiah 40:31) Waiting takes great faith.

I know you're saying to yourself, "but it is not that easy." I know all about this struggle. The struggle of not seeing what you believe God has promised you. When you cannot see it happening it can be very discouraging. When things look impossible it makes you want to totally give up. As I explained earlier, some days, my prayer was "Lord take away the desire to be a mother." I could not see how with a diagnosis of primary amenorrhea due to an absent uterus that I would one day receive the blessings of motherhood. Somehow, I mustered up the faith not to give up on God. Somehow, I believed the report of the Lord over the reports of the doctors.

When you think about who God is and how He is not like man that He should lie, you sit in expectation and press beyond what your situation looks like. Hannah pressed as she prayed in the temple for a child. She did not accept her current state of being bitter and childless. I knew if I was going to receive my blessing from the Lord, if I was going to inherit the treasure that I felt was mine, I had to wait, or at least die trying. There was going to be no other way I could live but to lie and wait for my blessing. I refused to accept my present condition.

Prayers for Fertility, Healing & Adoption

I want to encourage you to never give up on God. If it is IVF that is possible or available to you, I want to agree with you in prayer that God allows the right door to open. The finances and insurance coverage needed to utilize IVF will be provided, and that the patience and faith required for a successful transfer will fall upon you, in Jesus name! Even if there were unsuccessful cycles of IVF, I claim success in the next round. I believe God for your baby!

I want to touch and agree with you that if adoption is an option and a desire for you and/or your family, that you will align with the right agency at the right time for the right child. I pray that if this is God's will for you to become an adoptive parent that this route will be divinely revealed to you, in Jesus name! I believe God for your baby!

If a surrogate is needed in bringing forth God's child for you, I pray that the right vessel be made available and that the seed and surrogate be blessed in the name of Jesus. I believe God for your baby!

I want to pray for every man and woman whose reproductive organs are not functioning properly. I pray healing upon those organs, that sperm cells are shaped correctly, and sperm counts are high, eggs are fertilized, wombs are healthy, uterine linings are normal, fallopian tubes are normal, scar tissue is healed....I pray that blood pressure is normalized, weight is healthy, thyroid disease is no more, immune deficiency issues are irrelevant, ovulation is normal, and I come against uterine fibroids, endometriosis and any other disease that prevents God's people from being fruitful and multiplying. I believe God for your baby!

I pray that a child who needs a home, that you may be in close contact with, will be welcomed into your family's arms. I pray that if it is a child that is already born that God would have you to parent, that He will reveal that child to you and that you will be positioned correctly to receive that child into your home. I believe God for your baby!

I stand in agreement for anyone who fervently desires to bring forth life in this world, that God's will is to give you the desires of your heart, and that He blesses you beyond your wildest dreams and that you will experience the true joy of The Lord, when you look into the eyes of your child. No matter how He chooses to send the child, I believe God for your baby!

I believe. I believe God. I believe God for your baby!

Meditation Scripture:

"Now unto him that is able to do exceeding abundantly above all that we ask or think, according to the power that worketh in us."

-Ephesians 3:20 (KJV)

Prayer:

Father God, please help me with my unbelief. I know that it is impossible to please You without faith. So, God help me to have the faith needed to receive Your blessings. God, I thank You and I praise you now for my baby. I believe that You are able to do it, no matter what it may look like, I trust You. I surrender this burden to You and I know You will bless me indeed. Thank You, Lord! In Jesus name, Amen!

Song:

"He's Able" by Darwin Hobbs

Reflections

_____

_____

_____

_____

_____

_____

_____

_____

_____

_____

_____

_____

_____

_____

_____

_____

_____

_____

Chapter 5

THEY JUST DON'T GET IT

I have had to pray, on numerous occasions, a prayer of patience. My desire was not just for patience to wait for my baby but I needed patience to deal with people. If we can agree that children say the "darndest" things then we must know that adults can say the meanest and most insensitive things to a woman or couple who are struggling to conceive. I've had moments where I wanted to lash out in anger over the comments. Other times I wanted to cry out in despair but truth be told, I really wanted to make people understand that their words can make or break the day of someone who is infertile.

The reason I asked God for patience to deal with people is because I realized that many of my friends and family and even strangers that I

Your family and friends want you to succeed and most of them mean you well. encountered had no idea of the pain they were causing me by saying something about my condition. Even when someone would say the most hurtful things to me, The Lord helped me to understand that people who have never had issues with conception or miscarriage sometimes cannot identify with the issue. It is just like when someone loses a close loved one to an illness. Unless you have lost someone so close to you that you have sat on the front row at a funeral, it is difficult to identify with the pain and confusion that the person may be experiencing. I remember offering condolences to bereaved families as a consistent practice of mine. It was not until I sat on the front row at my grandmother's funeral that I understood the heaviness of that kind of loss. Now, I look at the people on the front rows at funerals from a new place of compassion. A place that I could not comprehend unless I experienced it for myself.

So, please do not be too hard on them! Your family and friends want you to succeed and most of them mean you well. The circle of people around you that are ignorant and lack compassion is a circle you need to run from. But there are others that genuinely love you and do not know how they can help you. I encourage you to have patience with folks and share this chapter with those you are surrounded by so they may first acknowledge that they do not understand your hurt and secondly, that they may change their vocabulary when speaking to you about your journey. Once they acknowledge their lack of understanding, this shows signs of humility which comes from a position of wanting to support. They want to help.

Here are some tips for loved ones that would like to offer support during the journey:

> *"Oh, it will happen for you, stop worrying."*
> This is a phrase that barren women hear far too often. We hear this when we have been trying for years and someone makes it sound so simple, as if pregnancy can happen with the snap of a finger. This saying is very insensitive and it denigrates their concern like they are overreacting. They were courageous enough to share

their heart with you, please do not give an oblivious reply such as this. A better way at giving advice is to say, "I believe God with you and I'm praying that He will give you direction." In most cases, women who share their heart regarding the issue of infertility really just need someone to listen. Hugs go a long way and can be much more comforting than words alone.

"Are you pregnant?"
If you know a woman has had issues with conception, do not, I repeat, do not ask her if she is pregnant. This phrase feels like a knife in the chest. Our one greatest desire is to become pregnant and give birth to a healthy baby. When you ask if we are and we are not, it is a reminder to us that once again we can't. A barren woman already feels ashamed but this question makes her feel less of herself. If your loved one becomes pregnant, they will share the news with you at the right time. Instead of asking if she's pregnant, ask her how she's doing. This will allow a conversation to open up and she may

choose to share or not. Keep praying for her but never ask her if she is pregnant. When she does conceive, she is probably still fearful and wants to keep the news to herself for the first trimester. Just wait, and when she shares the good news, rejoice with her and praise God with her!

"Maybe you're not supposed to have children."

I know true prophets are still in the land today and I also know that true prophets will never give the word of The Lord beginning with the word "maybe". Unless you have the gift of prophecy or hold the office of prophet and unless God released you to say this, we rebuke this phrase in the name of Jesus. We cannot afford for our faith to be waivered anymore so I will ask you ever so politely to speak that negative word over your own household. You are not God and you do not have the final say. This phrase can send a barren woman into a depression so deep that she questions her very own existence. Don't assist the enemy in putting negative thoughts into our heads. Instead say to your loved one "Although you may not understand now, God has a plan for your life." Encourage her to trust God.

"You're not getting any younger, you'd better hurry up"

I simply could not understand the ignorance of others, but the truth is they just don't get it. If you notice a woman who has been married for some time and has not given birth to children even though she seems to love children, she just might have fertility issues. I would advise that you would pause before opening up with this phrase. There is no other saying that I would recommend as an alternative but I would rather advise that you say nothing. Sometimes it is best to mind your own womb. Chances are, this woman has tried time and time again but has remained unsuccessful in a healthy pregnancy. When you utter a phrase like "You'd better hurry up!" in most cases she is already anxious and fearful that her biological clock is ticking and you are adding heaviness to her load. Don't use this phrase, ever.

"You want children? You can take mine (insert laughter)"

I know you were only trying to make her laugh because you did not know what to say. When you make a joke out of an issue that consumes her mind for most of her day, it can be very upsetting to the barren woman. Since you do have children, she may already have an underlying jealousy that lays dormant in her subconscious. This makes those envious feelings rise up in her to lash out on you, and it only makes her feel more sadness. Saying this phrase is like becoming her "Peninnah." This phrase is taunting even though you meant it as a joke. Instead you may want to share that you love your children and pray that she is soon allowed to experience the love of a child. Let her know that you love her and are praying with her.

"There's plenty of kids who need a home, why don't you just adopt?"

While adoption could be an option, some desire to conceive naturally. This question is not necessarily insensitive, but there is a proper way to ask this question. The better way to ask is "Have you considered adoption?" Some couples or individuals may not have the resources to adopt, some do not meet the qualifications to adopt, and some just never wanted to go that route. The way you ask this question could actually make them think about the option more seriously. Go the extra mile and research adoption agencies nearby and provide your loved one with their contact information. This will allow them to be able to at least think about the option which may lead to them meeting the child of their dreams.

"Did you get checked out yet?"

So, your loved one has been married for some years now, or your loved one is getting up in child-bearing age, so you blurt out this most oblivious inquiry because they have not borne children yet. Contrary to popular belief, barrenness is more common than people think. Getting checked out is something that they have probably already done. For me, I dreaded going to the doctor because I knew there was something wrong. For a family member or friend to ask, "Did you get checked yet?" is hurtful and it really sounds like you're prying more than trying to help. This question sounds like you're trying to get the latest gossip and will not help your loved one at all. Instead you can again, mind your own womb, and say nothing. The truth is, it is none of your business! This issue is so close to their heart and you should be gentle with those who are brokenhearted. Also, while adoption can be a great option, to the barren woman it sounds like you are saying, "Just give up already." Be sensitive, mind your own womb!

These are actual phrases that barren women have heard from their own family members, parents, grandparents, siblings, aunts, uncles, cousins, church family, and strangers from a survey I conducted. I believe our family and friends generally want to help and encourage us. Remember to speak life. Please do not feel pressure to say something. Sometimes, it is most appropriate to say nothing at all. A hug and a prayer can go a long way.

Meditation Scripture:
"So encourage each other and build each other up."

-I Thessalonians 5:11a (NLT)

Prayer:
Lord God help me to speak life over the people that need my encouragement. Even if I don't understand their sadness in the natural, God help me to understand it in the spirit. Help me to encourage with my words and my actions. Lord I pray for the right words to say at the right time. Use me to comfort your people and help us to continue to keep each other lifted in prayer as we face some of the most difficult situations of our lives. Help us to be sensitive to one another and let us walk in unity so we may touch and agree, join hands and hearts, believing that You will bless them and that you will bless me. In Jesus name, Amen!

Song:
"Touch and Agree" by Isaiah D. Thomas & Elements of Praise

Reflections

_____

_____

_____

_____

_____

_____

_____

_____

_____

_____

_____

_____

_____

_____

_____

_____

_____

_____

_____

Chapter 6
GET DRUNK

Yes, I am saved, sanctified, and filled with the Holy Ghost. And no, this is not, in any form, an invitation or an endorsement to consume any alcoholic beverages. I do not condone drinking alcohol to suppress the harsh realities we go through in life. But can I be honest. My issues with fertility has caused me in some seasons to get drunk to try and numb the pain and disguise the hurt I was feeling. It was not often, but I can recall some nights, pouring multiple glasses of wine to escape the childless life I was living. The numbing never lasted long and it would only cause more pain than the relief I was aiming for. If you have turned to liquor, drugs, promiscuous sex, or any other negative outlet that could lead to destruction, stop now! None of these substances will heal the hurt you are feeling. If you cannot stop on your own, please reach out for help. This is not what God wants for your life. I did not struggle with wine spirits for long, but what I did discover was that there was another spirit that I would need to tap into that would bring me beyond coping with my barren situation. It would help me to conquer it instead. The prayer of travail.

Travail is defined as a painful or laborious effort. To travail is to be engaged in an agonizing or arduous effort. The Prayer of Travail is a prayer of weeping and a prayer of struggle. It is a prayer of determination and a prayer of persistence. Travailing is not cute and it is not dignified. When we travail, we are crying out to God, pouring out our hearts from a painful place. There are times when the prayer of travail is not understood by others. In the book of 1 Samuel, our sister Hannah cried out to The Lord because of her grieving spirit:

> *"And she was in bitterness of soul, and prayed unto the Lord, and wept sore."*
> *-1 Samuel 1:10 (KJV)*

Hannah's travail came from a place of grief. The grief I felt from being childless was a daily, agonizing heartache I was living with. It was a heaviness that made me bitter, and like Hannah, I turned and I prayed to the Lord with tears that seem to come from my heart. If you have the privilege of waking up in the morning and facing this thing called life, chances are, there is something that has happened along the way that has caused you great anguish and has caused you to cry from the depths of your soul. I learned that God receives these liquid prayers from His children. He actually hears and sees them. I used to view crying as a sign of weakness. Crying has been a form of prayer for me for years now and I know that my tears are seen and heard by God. Go ahead and cry. Cry as often as you believe is needed. It can be difficult or embarrassing when you are not alone, but I encourage you to find a place to let it out. Let out a travailing cry from your soul.

Even Hannah was misunderstood as being drunk as she prayed a prayer of travail unto The Lord. What sense would it make to go to the Lord in prayer, knowing you want to cry, but trying to hold back your emotions in an attempt to be dignified or "proper" in His presence. God knows the very hairs on our heads. Go ahead and let it out. He is our Abba Father and we can cry in His presence. He understands our tears when we cannot even formulate words. Be honest with the Father when you're in His presence. He is all knowing and knows the truth anyway. If you're angry or confused, say so. I had to stop performing prayer and begin to be present in prayer.

Travailing prayer is not some hopeless emotional ritual with a word count requirement that is full of big phrases. It is an encounter with our Heavenly Father, prayed from one who is positioned in desperation, expecting God to answer, and focused on results. Be real with God. Have a little talk with Jesus. Don't perform in prayer, but rather pray in your language and pray in the spirit. He wants to hear your voice. When you are travailing in prayer from a place of turmoil or deep pain, it is groaning, crying, and screaming that becomes your genuine language. I've learned that it is my authentic voice that God responds to. In Matthew Chapter 6, Jesus is teaching on prayer. He gives the disciples a model for prayer, encouraging them to begin in worship, and not to stand in hypocrisy with empty phrases. Keep it real with God.

The Prayer of Travail is also persistent and fervent. This is the prayer that keeps being prayed until results are given. If someone has ever told you that you lack faith because you kept on praying for the same thing over and over again, please understand that they are dead wrong. The Bible teaches us to ask, seek, and knock. Let's examine Matthew 7:7-11:

> *"Ask, and it shall be given you; seek, and ye shall find; knock, and it shall be opened unto you: For every one that asketh receiveth; and he that seeketh findeth; and to him that knocketh it shall be opened. Or what man is there of you, whom if his son ask bread, will he give him a stone? Or if he ask a fish, will he give him a serpent? If ye then, being evil, know how to give good gifts unto your children, how much more shall your Father which is in heaven give good things to them that ask him?" (KJV)*

We learn here the importance of being persistent in prayer and that the love of God responds to our prayer requests, not because we deserve blessings, but rather because of God's mercy. Jesus gives the example of an earthly father. He's saying that even we give our children what they stand in need of. We do not turn down our children's requests even if we pause in our response. Our slow yes is given even after an abrupt no. All of humanity, having been born in sin, know how to give good gifts to our children. This is a natural order. How much more would a supernatural God give to the children He created Himself? Just because you have not seen the manifestation of what you have been asking from God does not mean you ought to stop asking.

Ask Him for what you desire. I know you have already asked, but ask again. And then ask some more. Begin to seek God, delight yourself in Him and He will give you the desires of your heart. The scripture says, "ask and it shall be given." Shall be given and not might be given. Don't be afraid to ask your Father for what you want. Most children ask their parents repeatedly for the same things until they get what they want.

When I tried to quit praying that prayer, Holy Spirit wouldn't allow it to happen. Imagine a 2-year-old boy lifting his toddler arms to his dad saying, "Up daddy, pick me up daddy." Even if dad was in pain, he would eventually pick up his baby because he'd be willing to suffer a little pain just to make his son's day. Oh, how much more does our Father in Heaven love us. He loves us so much that He sent His Son to die for us. God wants to heal your broken heart. Keep asking for what you want and don't give up.

You may be confused and unsure if what you're asking for is lined up in His plan for your life. I cannot tell you how many times I went back and forth in my head over this issue. At times, I didn't know if my prayers were hitting a brick wall because maybe it just wasn't in God's plans for me to be a mother. I had to rebuke that doubtful spirit. I encourage you to continuously seek His presence. Your desires will begin to align with His will as you seek first His Kingdom. When you are focused on finding God and seeking the thing that you so desire, you will find it.

And knock. I believe travailing is a knock in itself. When you knock on something, you are determined to see what's on the other side. When you knock, you are expecting to eventually walk through. I thank God for travail. I cried out to the Lord, sometimes not even saying words, but I would plead for the Lord to bless me with a child, being fervent and persistent. When I tried to quit praying that prayer, Holy Spirit wouldn't allow it to happen. It was like I did not have a choice. I needed this blessing and so I travailed before God for it.

Pray also in the Spirit. The Spirit will help you with that which is unknown and unidentified. Romans 8:26 says:

> *"Likewise the Spirit also helpeth our infirmities: for we know not what we should pray for as we ought: but the Spirit itself maketh intercession for us with groanings which cannot be uttered." (KJV)*

Not only do we pray for a child, but we pray for understanding, for deliverance, and for contentment. We pray for decision-making, for good health, for successful marriage, for a sane mind, and for a healed heart. Even when we don't know what to pray for. To build yourself up, I encourage you as the Apostle Paul does, to pray in the Spirit. We cannot always pray from a posture of understanding. Praying in the Spirit will pray for those things too deep for words. The infertility struggle is such a deep and painful journey that makes you question your very existence. But praying in the Holy Ghost will cover that which you do not understand and it will help you to edify yourself.

Cry from your soul, pray in the Spirit, and never stop asking God for your child.

Meditation Scripture:

"This poor man cried, and the _LORD_ _heard him, and saved him out of all his troubles._ _The angel of the_ _LORD_ _encampeth round about them that fear him, and delivereth them._ _O taste and see that the_ _LORD_ _is good: blessed is the man that trusteth in him._

-Psalm 34:6-8 (KJV)

Prayer:

Dear Lord, I cry out to you from the very depths of my soul. I do not understand why I am going through this. My heart is heavy and my spirit is grieved. I cry out to you Abba Father. Hear my prayer request God, and please bless me with a child. God please heal my broken heart. Lord deliver me from bitterness. God, I know you are good; please show your goodness in my barrenness. I love you Lord and at times I am confused. Help me. In Jesus name. Amen.

Song:

"Blessings" by Laura Story

Reflections

_____

_____

_____

_____

_____

_____

_____

_____

_____

_____

_____

_____

_____

_____

_____

Chapter 7
ELKANAH'S LOVE

When discussing infertility, most people overlook the men. The issue, at first thought, is considered a problem that women essentially deal with. But what about the men? In my experience, among the women and couples I have had conversations with expressed that men go through heartache and pain just as much as the women do. I cannot speak from the male perspective, but I know that my husband has suffered along with many other husbands who have needed to support their wives through infertility or have, in fact, had infertility problems of their own. We cannot forget about what men are going through. This infertility journey is shared between men and women. It does not discriminate. The concern is the same, even if the way in which the grief is expressed by a man may differ totally from the grief shown by a woman. By nature, we are emotionally different.

Our story is unlike no others I've heard. I remember the day I first shared with Allen that I could not have children. After dating for three years, we knew we wanted to eventually get married. We were still quite young but I knew I needed to share my secret with him before we got married. Allen's response to me, when I finally revealed my barren condition, was one I did not expect. He told me, "Honey, don't worry. We can adopt." I was so relieved to know that I had someone that loved me so much that he was willing to take this hurting journey with me. I thought this news would be a deal breaker. Yet, he decided to love me through it.

Our marriage is far from perfect. Allen is my best friend, and him being childless was just as heavy for him as it was for me. So, my heart was hurting for him as well as for myself. His biological mother passed away from a sudden illness when he and his twin brother were just a year old. They were adopted and experienced a loving mother through a woman by the name of Viola Bailey. Allen has shared so many stories with me about Mrs. Bailey that I feel like I knew her also. She took them in and loved them as her own. When Allen was just in the second grade, Mrs. Bailey lost her battle with cancer, leaving Allen, his brothers and the rest of the Bailey family without their matriarch. Allen lost a mother twice before he was 10 years old. He's always had big dreams of starting his own tribe, his own clan, with a woman who wanted children just as much as he did. So, my news of infertility was a mighty blow to say the least. But he still stood by my side. We stood by each other, which is the key to survival.

Pray for him like you need him to pray for you.

I believe standing by each other is the key. Infertility support is not simply the husband supporting the wife, but it is both spouses helping one another through. Marriage is a partnership. Some days, Allen was strong for me. He would find me crying and just wrap his arms around me. Other days I had to encourage him that we would be parents one day. We cannot forget about the men. They also stand in the need of prayer. Men are just as excited and nervous when the pregnancy test reads positive. They are just as disappointed when the pregnancy test is negative. Men are just as devastated at the news of a miscarriage. They hurt just as much as we do. Praying together will strengthen your relationship and help you both to understand that you are in this thing together. Sisters, I encourage you to pray for your spouse in your private prayer time. He needs to be encouraged, he needs strength for this journey, and he needs the patience to deal with it all. Pray for him like you need him to pray for you.

I've seen how my infertility made my husband so vulnerable. Good men are providers and protectors. A good man wants to shield his woman from anything that might hurt her. This is the nature of anyone who loves someone. However, infertility is a problem that neither of you have control over. Allen was frustrated because he could not physically fix it for me. He wanted to help me and he encouraged me to go to the gynecologist. I despised going to the doctor because I just knew it was not possible. I would avoid calling to make appointments and I'd even make excuses to miss my appointments. Allen would stay on me, making sure I kept my Ob/Gyn appointments. He would even go with me whenever I had an appointment. Essentially, it was because of his persistence that I was able to finally receive a diagnosis of primary amenorrhea. Allen encouraged me, that if we went to the doctor we could get some answers. I didn't want to hear the doctor say no, while Allen wanted to hear the doctor say why. He was so optimistic that we would have children, no matter how it came to be. Later, his actions would both hurt me and bless me.

> *"Whenever the day came for Elkanah to sacrifice, he would give portions of the meat to his wife Peninnah and to all her sons and daughters. But to Hannah he gave a double portion because he loved her, and the Lord had closed her womb."*
>
> *-1 Samuel 1:4-5 (NIV)*

Elkanah loved his wife Hannah, despite her inability to give him children. She was given a double portion from her husband. He loved her through her condition and she loved him just as much. Elkanah was concerned about his wife when she was downhearted and would not eat but he did not abandon her, divorce her, or dismiss her. Hannah still remained in his household as the wife he so loved. Infertility did not outweigh the passion he possessed for his beloved.

Hannah was put in a predicament that reminded her daily that another woman was able to have children with her husband while she could not. I did mention earlier that my marriage was anything but perfect. I want to be as transparent as possible because I need the world to understand how God will use the most hurtful circumstances to bring you just the opposite: joy! I believe Allen struggled with the idea of not having children so much that his next move put my feelings on the backburner. He decided to have a child with another woman. And he hid it from me for over a year. I didn't hear about it from another person but he sat me down and poured out his heart to me that he'd been secretly taking care of his son and that he never meant to hurt me. I have never been slashed by a knife in a fight, but I swear those words cut deeper than any knife could - a barren woman whose husband just revealed to her that he cheated and got another woman pregnant. I thought this type of thing happens on soap operas or to other people, but there's no way this could happen to Allen and Najiyyah. This cannot be my life.

Can I be honest again? After my initial feelings of shock and anger, I was happy for him. I knew better than anyone what childlessness felt like. For the love of my life to be free from the bondage that infertility creates, I was genuinely excited for him. I know, you're thinking I'm crazy. But when you love someone unconditionally, you truly want them to have the desires of their heart. I even felt stupid, for several reasons. How did I not notice that he was gone so much? How could I be happy for him? I still don't fully understand the answers to these questions. I know now that God was setting me up for something.

Hannah would receive a double portion from Elkanah because of her closed womb. I felt at this point in our marriage, Allen gave double the effort to show how much he loved me. It took many years for me to forgive him, but I was able to do it. Through much prayer and effective communication our marriage survived the infertility and infidelity that almost destroyed it. Through this, our love grew even deeper for one another. We had heated arguments, was on the verge of divorce, and I was ready to give up. Somehow, some way, God made a way for us to fall even deeper in love. The Lord has restored trust and has healed the brokenness of barrenness and betrayal.

While we were trying to figure out where we stood in our marriage, I became a stepmother. A title I never thought I'd have, but ironically, I accepted the role immediately. The day after Allen revealed his secret to me, I met Jacob. A handsome 16-month old, who upon meeting me climbed on my lap and rested his head on my chest as if he already loved me. Jacob looked just like his daddy, he looked how I imagined our son would look like. Something happened to me that day. I bonded immediately with him, and began to treat him as if he was my own. When I looked at Allen, I would get angry and sad. But when I saw Jacob, I was filled with happiness. I was able to get a sneak peek at motherhood when he was with us.

This is my story. I know that for many couples trying to conceive, facing the issue of children being conceived out of adultery may not have been your dilemma. Overall, marriages are generally tried through the fire in addition to your fertility struggle. It could be a financial issue, a disagreement on adoption or medical treatment options. A fight about not getting enough emotional support from each other or simply an argument because you're both frustrated and tired of being childless. Whatever you may be facing with your spouse know that marriages are important to God. What He has joined together, let no man separate. Let no issue break you apart, let nothing come between you. This ride can be troubling, but God is present in your trouble. If God could restore Allen and I, I know He can do it for you.

Meditation Scripture:

"God is our refuge and strength, a very present help in trouble. Therefore will not we fear."
-Psalm 46:1-2a

Prayer:

Lord I thank You for being a present help in our time of trouble. Our childlessness feels like our earth shaking and oceans rising, but we thank You for being our help. Lord I pray for my spouse. Please mend our broken hearts and give us the patience to wait on you and to wait on each other. Let us communicate effectively with one another. Lord I pray for a healthy marriage, full of love, loyalty, comfort and peace. I come against anything that seeks to divide us. Use this issue of infertility to draw us closer to You and to one another. I love you and trust You Lord. In Jesus name, Amen.

Song:

"You Are My Strength," By Hillsong United

Reflections

_____

_____

_____

_____

_____

_____

_____

_____

_____

_____

_____

_____

_____

_____

_____

_____

_____

Chapter 8

LORD REMEMBER ME

In her deep anguish Hannah prayed to the Lord, weeping bitterly. And she made a vow, saying, "Lord Almighty, if you will only look on your servant's misery and remember me, and not forget your servant but give her a son, then I will give him to the Lord for all the days of his life.

-1 Samuel 1:10-11 (NIV)

This prayer was my prayer. Lord remember me. A prayer with only three words yet a complete prayer. It gets right to the point. Like Hannah I prayed this prayer from a place of grief and sadness. It was a prayer that I prayed out of desperation. I knew only the Almighty God could turn this situation around for me.

You've heard how unworthy I felt and how I dealt with feeling less of a woman because of my status. I have written about how I felt so low that I did not want to live anymore. I've told you about how I doubted that motherhood would ever happen for me with a diagnosis of primary amenorrhea. Yet, I still prayed that the Lord would remember me. And He did! Let me tell you how good God is.

As I was dealing with my husband's infidelity I found comfort in being a stepmother during times in which Jacob spent the night or weekends with us. I was able to experience, on a part-time basis, the joys of motherhood. I changed diapers, fixed meals, played peek-a-boo, and sang "Wheels on the Bus" many days. I loved it! Yet, I still felt the emptiness of childlessness. Perhaps it was because I always had to say goodbye to him when the weekend was over. It may have been that I was embarrassed for what Jacob represented - another woman was able to give my husband a child when I could not. It was eating me up inside but I could not deny the fact that I was still in love with my husband and trying to be brave enough to work things out and trust him again.

Jacob was now two-years-old and our bond had grown quite a bit. I recall one day as we were in our apartment, he was running around playing and then he fell and bumped his knee. He began to cry so I ran to help and comfort him. Before I picked him up, he looked up at me from the floor and said with tears in his eyes, "Mommy." I said, "Allen, I think Jake is crying for his mother." I looked at him again and he repeated to me in his toddler dialect, "Mommy, it hurt." The happiness I felt in that moment is unexplainable. This was the very first time I was called "Mommy." I had been a wife, a daughter, a sister, and an auntie, but never a mom. I became Jacob's other mother in that moment and it is a memory that I will never forget. My husband and I never prompted Jacob to call me mommy. I treated him as if he were my own and I believe he must have felt a mother's love when he was with me, so he started calling me mommy on his own.

Adjusting to the role of stepmother while getting comfortable with sharing this new role with the world was perplexing. I was excited to be a mom, yet I was still embarrassed about how it came to be. Everyone knew that Allen and

Najiyyah had been together since high school. It was difficult enough to explain to our families. Although I knew I didn't owe anyone an explanation, it still felt weird. Nevertheless, I loved being Jacob's stepmother but still felt the emptiness of not having my own. At this point, I asked God was this the child He promised me. I wanted to know so I could know how to pray going forward. I didn't want to continue to pray for a child if this was the one. If Jacob was the way to motherhood, I was willing to accept it, even in its limitations.

Even though Jacob had filled my heart with joy, my heart was still broken. I continued with my prayer, "Lord, remember me." A couple more years went by, and I was still childless. In anguish, I kept praying. I would even ask God, "Is there something I have done to deserve this?" Sometimes we ask God crazy things like that. But God would still whisper in my ear, "Just wait." I was so frustrated! I wanted to know how long it would be. It was killing me.

In 2011, I lost my grandmother. The woman who raised me since I was 4 years old had a fatal heart attack. I arrived first on the scene before the paramedics got there and I had to watch my grandmother take her last breath. To say I felt tormented is an understatement. Not only was I childless and working on a broken marriage, but to add to the devastation I lost the only person left on earth that I knew loved me unconditionally. At this point I figured that nothing would go well for me. I was so grieved in 2011. My husband would often come home from work and find me in the corner of a room, on the floor weeping. I felt hopeless yet continued to pray, "Lord please, remember me."

That summer, our women's ministry held a retreat in the Poconos Mountains. This trip was right on time, about four weeks after my grandmother's funeral. I needed to get away and press into the presence of God. We had a rededication service during the retreat. The leader of our women's ministry, the late great Reverend Danielle E. Bush, asked me to minister in dance during the dedication. She said that the Lord showed her me dancing as they handed out the white scarves to the women. So, I went forth in the dance and I ministered to a song by Ricky Dillard that uttered a simple phrase:

Our Father
You are Holy
We give you glory
And we bless Your name

These four lines sang over and over allowed for the women to press into God's presence. It simply states who God is and that all glory belongs to Him. When you begin to bless God, everything else you're dealing with seems so small in comparison. That day I danced freely, with no choreography prepared. I just simply worshipped and it was an experience I will never forget.

After the rededication ceremony, Reverend Bush prophesied to me. She said to me, "Najiyyah you've been asking God when will you be happy. The Lord says in 2011, you will have joy, peace and happiness." I received the word of the Lord and I waited in expectancy. I even picked up a rock while we were in the Poconos before we left and wrote down the words on the rock: joy, peace, happiness 2011. I believed God would bless me. Summer turned into fall, and fall into winter. I was still childless and in grief.

A young lady whom served in ministry with me asked if my husband and I would be the godparents of her daughter. We gladly accepted the responsibility, even though we were not so close. I was honored to be a godmother. This would make godchild number 3 for Allen and me.

On New Year's Eve, after we counted down to midnight at my church's Watch Night worship service, I was depressed. I looked to God in prayer as I went home that night in disappointment. I said, "God you told me through your prophetess that I would have joy, peace and happiness in 2011. It is after midnight, what gives? God what happened? Do you still love me? Did I miss the blessing? Please help me! I'm so confused!"

As my new year began, I tried to move on. Yet I felt in my spirit, that I was supposed to be a mom. So, I continued to pray, "Lord, remember me." One day I overheard a conversation between my goddaughter's aunt and grandmother. They were asking for prayer for my goddaughter's mother who seemed to be struggling with taking care of her newborn. So, as the godparent, I asked if I could help. I reached out to her mom and she agreed, after I spoke to Allen about it, that Baby Tameekah would stay with us for a little while. The idea initially was to allow her mom some time to get herself together. I picked up my goddaughter on a Saturday in May, brought her home and prepared to be her caretaker for a little while.

She was just four months old and the happiest baby I'd ever seen. Initially, I didn't want to get too attached because I thought she'd be returning to her mom. Months rolled by, and she was still with us. Her mom allowed us to get custody of her since it would be more of a longer term than we first expected. We went to the courthouse together and filed the paperwork. I still didn't quite understand what was happening. One night while I was putting Tameekah to sleep, singing "Rock-a-bye Baby," I remembered that she was born on December 30, 2011. I got the revelation as I gazed into her peaceful, sleeping face that the joy, peace and happiness that God had promised was indeed delivered before the end of 2011, just as it was prophesied to me! I began to cry and said, "God, is this the baby you promised me?" I heard a clear "yes" from the Lord and I rejoiced with my sleeping child in my arms.

I was in awe! I am still in awe of how God moved. I was afraid at first, but then God continued to reassure me that this was the child I prayed for. The Lord remembered me as He remembered Hannah. I knew this was the promised child because one day I looked around and realized that the hurt I once felt was gone. The anguish of childlessness was over! After all those years of heartache, I genuinely felt that I was officially delivered from those emotions. I thought that only a biological child would satisfy the hunger of motherhood. But let me tell you that our God is AMAZING! He has completely blown my mind with this.

Every infirmity including infertility must bow down to the God of Abraham, Isaac and Jacob.

If God has made a way for this barren woman to become a mother, He can do anything! He will make a make a way in the wilderness, and rivers in the desert. Every infirmity including infertility must bow down to the God of Abraham, Isaac and Jacob. God has redeemed us and we are precious and honored in His sight. Even as we go through the waters of the unknown He is with us. As we go through fear and hurt, He is with us. As we walk through the fires of disappointment, we shall not be burned. When we face the overwhelming reality of barrenness, it will not overtake us.

If you love God and believe in Him, that means He has called you by name. You belong to Him and He loves you. There is nothing my God cannot do. He is bigger than any situation. The Almighty is greater than anything we can imagine. I am surrounded by children! I am blessed beyond my wildest dreams, and it was God who did it all! Look to the Lord and know that the God of heaven and earth holds the most precious things in His hands. To Him be all the glory, all the honor and all the praise.

Meditation Scripture:

"Who hath measured the waters in the hollow of his hand, and meted out heaven with the span, and comprehended the dust of the earth in a measure, and weighed the mountains in scales, and the hills in a balance? Lift up your eyes on high, and behold who hath created these things, that bringeth out their host by number: he calleth them all by names by the greatness of his might, for that he is strong in power; not one faileth."

-Isaiah 40:12,26

Prayer:

Lord remember me. Help me. Bless me. Keep me. I will bless Your name forever.

Song:

"My God is Big," by Full Gospel Baptist Church Fellowship International Ministry of Worship

Reflections

Chapter 9

UNSPEAKABLE JOY

Joy is defined as a feeling of great pleasure. It is described as the emotion evoked by a sense of well-being, success, or good fortune. Joy, by the world's standards is considered to be a result of possessing what one desires. In other words, joy by the world's definition can only happen when we have everything we want. Joy is usually associated with achievement of some sort, it is connected with doing something, finding something, or getting something. To have joy is to be delighted, to be glad, to be in a state of happiness or a state of extreme gratification and satisfaction. So, it's safe to say that most have joy when life is good and everything is perfect. It is expected that we would have joy and be exceedingly glad when everything is going good, but for the believer we can have joy even when we get a bad report from the doctor. The believer can have joy even when a negative diagnosis is given. We can have joy even after getting a being disappointed, after a failed pregnancy test, or even after a miscarriage. The truth of the matter is that our days are few and full of trouble, but there's good news: This joy that I have, the world didn't give it to me, the world didn't give it and the world can't take it away.

In Galatians 5:22-23 it is written:

"But the fruit of the Spirit is love, joy, peace, forbearance, kindness, goodness, faithfulness, gentleness and self-control." *(NIV)*

Webster defines joy as a condition or feeling of high pleasure or delight, but this joy that Paul is referring to in Galatians is a fruit of the Holy Spirit. You can still praise God while struggling with infertility. Some days are very heavy and people may notice you down one day and praising God the next day. They may wonder how it's possible for you to have joy in sorrow. I have joy now but I had joy even in childlessness. I have joy because I have the Holy Ghost. It says in verses 24 and 25 of Galatians 5:

> *"And they that are Christ's have crucified the flesh with the affections and lusts. If we live in the Spirit, let us also walk in the Spirit."* *(KJV)*

The fruit of joy has manifested in you, so come hell or high water you will never lose your joy because this joy that you have, the world did not give it to you.

We are encouraged in Galatians chapter 5 that joy, along with the other fruits of the Spirit, is a direct result of living and walking in the Spirit. Joy in sorrow is not just a lyric in a gospel song, no. It is not just a nice church saying, but joy in sorrow is possible because of Jesus. Joy is unlike happiness, because happiness depends on what happens in my life, this joy is totally reliant on my relationship with God. Jesus says in John 15:5:

> *"I am the vine, you are the branches, He who abides in Me and I in him, bears much fruit.*

For without Me, you can do nothing."
(NASB)

Jesus is telling us that He is our source, He is the true vine. If we stay connected to Him, we naturally bear spiritual fruit. If I abide in God, He shall abide in me. When I stay connected to God, no matter what happens, I can still have joy.

In chapter 15 of John's gospel, Jesus is teaching us how to stay connected to Him and in verse 11 He says:

> *"these things I have spoken to you that my joy remain in you and that your joy might be full." (ESV)*

The scripture specifically says that His joy may remain in us. This joy lights up any darkness, this joy can never be overcome with sorrow, even the heaviness of infertility. Jesus promised that despite what we would have to face in this life, that if we abide in Him, He would make our joy full. We abide in him by reading His word. We abide in Him by talking to Him every day through prayer. Communication equals connection.

James 1:2 says that you should:

"Count it all joy when you fall into various trials." (ESV)

John Maxwell says in his commentary of this scripture, "we can find joy in the midst of problems only when we recognize their purpose and results." God loves us so much and He wants the best for us. God has divine plans for us to prosper and not to harm us. Jesus said that He came that we might have life more abundantly. Although our trials will come, be encouraged because ALL things work together for good to them that love God to them who are the called according to his purpose. Do you love Him today? Are you called according to His purpose? Then count it all joy! Joy will come even in the hardest times of your life. Joy is already here for you.

Know that joy is a fruit manifested by the Holy Spirit, remember that joy is a result of connection, and also remember to count it all joy! This joy that I have, this joy that we have, is a joy that is way down in our souls. It is a sweet, soul-saving joy that is not compromised by the things of this world. I get unspeakable joy when I think about what God has done in my life. I believe that God will do the same thing for you. Whatever you desire from the Lord, delight yourself in Him and He will give you the desires of your heart. In His presence, there is fullness of joy, at His right hand there are pleasures forevermore. God bless you.

Meditation Scripture:

"You make known to me the path of life; you will fill me with joy in your presence, with eternal pleasures at your right hand.

-Psalm 16:11

Prayer:

Father God, help me to dwell in your presence so that I may experience Your joy. I worship You God, in spirit and in truth, in the beauty of holiness. I know that you are a big God. You are bigger than my infertility. I draw near to you Father. Help me to keep my mind on You in spite of what I've been through. You are strong God and You are mighty and I know Your plans for me goes beyond my wildest dreams. You are good God and You are good to me. I'll stay connected to You! I'll put on the garment of praise for my spirit of heaviness because You have given it to me. I know that my weeping may endure for a night but joy will come in the morning. You are the rock on which I stand. I love You and I trust You! In Jesus name, Amen!

Song:

"I Smile," by Kirk Franklin

Reflections

_____

_____

_____

_____

_____

_____

_____

_____

_____

_____

_____

_____

_____

_____

_____

_____

CONCLUSION

A testimony is a formal statement that is written or spoken to prove or disprove a claim. I have shared my testimony so that others may witness what God has done in my life. I made a promise to God, that if He would bless me to be a mother I would tell everyone, everywhere I go. I could not keep this story to myself. I pray that is has encouraged you. I believe that no matter what your story is, this story is relatable. How many times have we made plans that have not played out the way we thought they should? How many issues have slipped beyond our control? We have all experienced something along our journeys that rocked us to the point that all we could do was l

I also want to share that while writing this book, my family experienced a crisis that no one could have foreseen. We could have lost my husband due to a horrific violent crime. Innocently standing by, on his way home to his wife and children, bullets that were not even intended for him entered his body. While some people have died due to one gun shot, my husband survived multiple gunshot wounds. God has protected and provided. He is a healer and a keeper!

As I tended to my family and as we recovered from this tragedy, God gave me the strength to continue to write this book. When God gives you a word, you must release it in season. God can do anything! He has kept me since I was in my mother's womb:

- He prevented the abortion my mother had planned.
- He provided me a safe and loving upbringing when my mother was unable to care for me.
- He was and is a Father to me, a fatherless child.
- He saw me through a reckless and sinful lifestyle in my teen and young adult years.
- He reminded me that He loved me when I wanted to end my life.

- He comforted me when I lost my grandmother.
- He gave me strength to care for my dying mother.
- He broke the chain of despair over my childlessness.
- He restored my marriage after infidelity.
- He spared my husband's life and healed his body.
- He blessed me with two little ones that call me Mommy.

I cannot list all of the things God has done for me, I would be writing for years. The greatest of them all, God gave me the gift of salvation and the gift of the Holy Spirit.

If you do not know The Lord, Jesus, Yeshua Hamashiach, as your personal Savior, get to know Him today. God sent His Son, Jesus, to die on a cross for your sins and my sins, that we would be free from death. If you believe in the Son, the Redeemer, you will have victory: an abundant life here on earth and eternal life in heaven. All you have to do is admit to God that you are a sinner, believe that He died, was raised from the dead and is coming back again, and confess Him as your Lord and Savior. It's that simple.

Life as a believer is not always peachy. In fact, the enemy (Satan) desires to destroy you. But as a believer, you are covered by the blood of Jesus. My entire life is a witness of that covering. Come to know Him and you will see for yourself.

For my sisters and brothers in Christ, stay encouraged throughout this Christian journey. Although you may suffer, know that these present sufferings are not worthy to be compared with the glory that shall be revealed in you. God bless you all.

RESOURCES

There are several resources that are available for infertility support. I have personally used the following resources listed below. They have given me encouragement and hope on my most emotional days. I pray these will bless you as they have blessed me. Most of them are free of charge and provide services that are confidential.

Sarah's Laughter

Christian Support for Infertility and Child Loss

This non-profit organization is committed to providing support to couples struggling with infertility, miscarriage or child loss. I signed up for their Daily Double Portions, a daily encouragement based on God's word to help you along your journey.

www.sarahs-laughter.com

Dancing Upon Barren Land
Spiritual Nourishment for the Infertility Road

This is an organization who also offers infertility support. They take prayer request and have a blog that gives fertility facts and spiritual encouragement for couples and women. You can sign up for Fertility Fact Friday and receive info on fertility via email.

www.dancinguponbarrenland.com

Resolve
The National Infertility Association

This national resource can point you in the direction of local support groups in your state. Learn about adoption and other infertility awareness events nationally.

www.resolve.org

Hannah's Prayer Ministries
Christian Support for Fertility Challenges

The founder of this ministry, Jennifer Saake, has written a book based on biblical principles of faith as it relates to infertility. They also have a prayer community offering prayer and encouragement for women and men.

www.hannah.org

SPONSORS & ASSOCIATES

The following individuals have partnered with me to ensure that the message of Hannah's Heart reaches the masses.

Special thanks to the following Sponsors:

Octavia Bradley, CTA

In His Hands Travel Agency
732-334-8458
Inhishandstravel1@gmail.com

Theresa Berryman

Author of *Thou Shalt Also Decree A Thing*
www.theresaberryman.com

Marguerita Cooper

Anointed Seamstress & Owner of Mantles For Ministry
Ritahatcher234@yahoo.com

Cynthia Frazier

Author of *God's Plan, Not Mine*
www.cynthiahughesfrazier.com

Keisha Harris-Watson

Minister of Dance & Liturgical Dance Instructor
Keishah_1982@yahoo.com

Sheena Johnson

Sponsor

Shaquana Jordan

Co-Founder of DEW Ministries
Founder of Movement That Ministers
CEO of Free Indeed Center for Dance
www.ShaquanaJordan.com

Stephanie Shider

Author of *I Think I Like My Natural Hair,*
CEO of Lady on A Mission/Girls On A Mission
www.ladyonamission.org

Special thanks to the following Associate Partners:

Delana Barno

Melanie Byrd

Maria Camino

Annette Don Martin

Pamela Edwards

Denaea Lawrence

Princess Johnson

ABOUT THE AUTHOR

Najiyyah Bailey

Najiyyah Bailey is a native of Plainfield, NJ. She is a faithful member of Ruth Fellowship Ministries in Plainfield under the leadership of Senior Pastor, Rev. Tracey L. Brown. Najiyyah serves in several capacities at her church. She is a founding member and Director of the Anointed Earthen Vessels Dance Ministry, whose mission is to be a blessing to the church and community, sharing the gospel and encouraging the Body of Christ through dance.

Najiyyah discovered her love of writing and teaching while studying English at Fairleigh Dickinson University. Studying to show herself approved, Najiyyah has completed theological studies in the areas of dance, leadership and prayer. She is also the co-founder of DEW Ministries, a NJ-based community dance ministry whose focus is on evangelism and uniting & educating liturgical dancers and worship artists.

Najiyyah is a graduate of New Brunswick Theological Seminary, receiving a Certificate in Theological Studies. In the marketplace, she is the owner of Butterfly East Graphic Design and co-owner of Divine Divas Events, Inc.

Najiyyah is the wife of her high school sweetheart, Allen Bailey and they are the parents of Jacob and Tameekah. She is wholeheartedly grateful to the Lord for allowing her to be a wife and mother. Her desire is to abide in God, so that He may abide in her. Najiyyah enjoys studying the word of God and she loves to teach others what the Word says, discovering God's truth. It is her desire to share those discoveries with others, to see people transformed by the word of God, and to spread the good news of the Gospel of Jesus Christ through the many gifts He has given her.

Najiyyah is committed to advancing the Kingdom of God through song, dance, prayer, and the preached word. **Hannah's Heart** is her first published work.

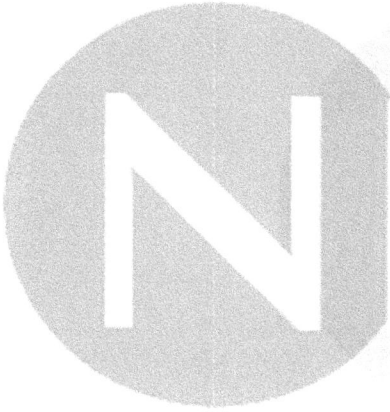

Stay connected with Najiyyah at:

www.NajiyyahBailey.com

@HannahsHeartByNajiyyah